Find the good.

Edited by Sunni Soper
& Christopher Michael
Cover Art by June The Trillustrator

Published By

Printed in the United States of America
ISBN 978-0-9984270-9-6
Published by 310 Brown Street
www.310brownstreet.com
imanitrishawn@gmail.com

Artwork has a way of memorializing where you are in a specific moment. Sometimes it is about proving that these things happened because you feel as though the world will keep moving and your memories won't be enough. I married young; Call it stupid, call it naïve – I called it love. I am now divorced and have since learned the value of knowing and fully loving yourself before trying to build a life with someone. Call it a hard lesson.

We are taught to search for love from a young age. We watch fairytales and romanticize relationships in search of happily ever after. However, most of us don't experience healthy loving relationships in our own homes growing up so we are sent into the world stumbling through heartbreaks, trying our best. We never do the work to make ourselves whole; therefore, we offer all that we have, often not leaving anything for ourselves. You can't give what you don't have. This is a collection of love poems, some beautiful, some painful.

I have had enough poems to publish for years now but nothing felt important enough, good enough to give to the world. I decided when I  was 19 that I would live my life out loud, share with the world this journey I'm on and unfortunately, that means the hard stuff too. I hope this work blesses you, heals you, and moves you. I hope you know we were made for love but we can only love others as well as we love ourselves.

To the hearts I broke while trying to rebuild my own, I am sorry. I loved you with all I had and it wasn't enough. Here's to us being young and loving fearlessly. Here's to us learning to do it the right way. Here's to us loving again... one day.

"And in the end, we were all just humans…
Drunk on the idea that love, only love, could heal our
brokenness."
~F. Scott Fitzgerald

Dad Says,

Don't dilute yourself into thinking that this book is not about him.

Dad says,
It's your journey, but you didn't take it alone.

Dad says,
You have washed your hands of the guts, but he is still bleeding.

Dad says,
He dusted you off and called you diamond, but I had been teaching you about settings for years.

Dad says,
It's not that I didn't like him, I just saw you when you didn't see yourself and some people aren't equipped to hold something so big.

Dad says,
I love you. But he means, I am sorry, I wish I could have protected you from this heartbreak. Your head has always been hard, I told you your bottom was softer. When you gon' get sick of learning the hard way, Mo?

Dad says,
You'll be fine.

I say I know.

Dear Diary,

I'm scared this searching
spirit and heart of mine won't honestly settle down. Just play the role
for a time. Merely invite someone along for the ride.

A Leap of Faith

I've been a fool often
I've fallen for things that shined,
That glittered
The idea of love has always been far more pleasant than the act
Similar to gold
I attain my best value melted down
In dark rooms
Beneath tear stained pillows
In uncomfortable pews
Atop scabbed knees and tattered bibles
We are all just searching for someone whose demons play with ours
Someone more interested in the flesh colored stories of the past than
our skeletons
Press your ear to my rib cage
Tell me what you feel
Tell me that these ribs, these were the ones that God removed from
you
And then from dirt, made me
Tell me that we are divine
That we are meant to be
Protect me from the shrapnel of my past mistakes
Tangle me in your strings
Let me fall for you
Let me play host to your love story
Please be the beauty to my beast of a heart
Glass slipper your way around my insecurities
Remind me that costumes are only for Halloween
If you ask me to
I'll lay it all down
For you

How Many Hearts Did You Break Before You Found Love?

Sometimes I think it's easier to be alone
From whom do you learn love?
I know the answer should be God
But I need something more tangible
I am scared that I am doomed to repeat what I know isn't love
Or I guess what I hope isn't love
In my mind
Love is selfless
Something you are willing to swallow yourself whole for
That euphoria
But what if the little things turn to big things
And scares the love away
Do you think love is shaky like that?
I just mended this heart
Found all the pieces
Ripped them from the hands of lovers who never deserved them
From younger versions of myself stone scarred in the crevasses of my
memory
I have never seen healed,
Seen healthy
But I think this is what it looks like
How many tears do you cry before you realize your cheeks aren't
made for salt?
I want a love that is extraordinary
Good enough isn't good enough in love
I want a lasting love
I am no longer scared of heartbreak
I'm scared of wasting my time
Of missing a lesson
Sometimes, I just need to be held
Is this love or am I mislabeling feelings?
I can't tell you
I've never seen love up close
Never seen someone give themselves away

Maybe that's my problem

I'm looking for something I've never seen
Solving a puzzle without first looking at the picture
I am more than my scars and bruises
More than my sad stories and abusers
I am this heart
Whatever that may be
I am this love
If that means anything at all
I am all of me
I guess I've just been waiting to give it away
But this time
To someone that deserves me
This smile
These tears
This laugh
All this care
I just hope I'm at least looking the right way

Falling

You won't feel it coming
Won't notice the moment they become a part of you
The moment you're willing to sacrifice your solitude for their presence
You will merely wake up one day and know that this is your new
normal
And know that matters of the heart are now infinitely more important
than logic

Caught

We are so reckless in love
We go into things heart first
Or we don't
And maybe that's the problem
We are never on the same page
We are fond of the term "first love"
I don't believe in that
That implies that there was someone before,
And there will be someone after
I have loved a few
But none like this
None like you
In all honesty infatuation is probably a better description
Because I wasn't in it like I am this
Wasn't okay with their permanence like I am yours
I have always been fond of finding escape routes
Never being too invested
Yet here I am
Here we are
And I am okay with that
Fine in the stability
Both feet fully planted

I Realize

I can't teach you how to love me
There is no how-to guide
I can't tell you when you see me falling apart to pick me up and put
me back together
Because you've probably never witnessed a hurricane like this
But even fools know to take cover when the rain hits
I can't explain to you in elaborate detail how on Valentine's Day
I want you to bring me a bouquet of flowers
Any kind
Preferably the cheaper ones
And plan to show me just how much I mean to you
How my voice gives you goosebumps
How I have a death grip on your heart
Not because it's Valentine's Day
Well
Maybe, because it's Valentine's Day
But most importantly because you know how much sentimental means
to me
I can't teach you how to love me
I can't tell you that when I'm borderline tears
And tell you to leave
That you must force yourself to stay
I can't explain to you
That on days
When I want nothing more than to be hidden
You must see me
You asked me why I loved you
And I told you that you made me happy
And that answer didn't suffice for you
But you see,
For so long happiness has been a dream
So please understand
When I say you make me happy

I mean tears no longer want to leave my eyes because they want a
front row view
You are more than I could have ever theorized
Because I've prayed for you
For so long
I can't teach you how to love me
I can't say that I'm easy
Because I'm sure other girls are less trouble
But in a world suffocated with dark clouds
You are my sunshine

I Have Never Made a Decision Based on Love

I find love to be a shaky ground
A brittle foundation
Too many things have been done to me in the name of love
So this is new
You are new
I can finally admit I'm scared
Admit that I'm looking in the mirror and seeing someone different
Someone new, staring back at me
And liking what I see
The person I'm becoming
I'm not going to say you're the reason
But I'm not saying you aren't
I am giving you my unknown
Believing that this time love can be trusted

What's It Like to Love a Ghost?

To see them there, but not feel them there
What's it like to tell someone goodbye knowing that they have already left?
I have never seen myself or loved myself from the outside
But I wonder if it is different loving me now
Is it easier to love someone who loves themselves?
Or is it the same?
Do you love as hard as you can regardless of how this person feels?
Some say my fiancé is like Superman
That he calls himself Clark Kent only to superhero save me from the depths of my own sorrow

I don't miss you anymore
I don't even talk to you
I don't think you're dangerous that way anymore, but I'd rather not take the chance
You were in love with my dark side
Read these words almost as if you had written them yourself
I remember stealing your shirts only so I could cry into your arms at night
We weren't good for each other
I know you've heard I'm getting married

I'm sorry

But depression,

Stop calling me

I have no more love to give

I Pray You Never Lose the Power to Take My Breath Away

That I never forget there are moments so powerful they leave me
speechless
I pray that when the enamor wears off
We've built a strong enough foundation to survive
This is merely the beginning of a lifetime with my best friend
I hope that when times get rough that we remember
That at our core
We are merely friends who decided to spend the rest of our lives
together
I hope that honesty is the overarching theme of our relationship
That twenty years from now
You still make me nervous
I still stare at you when you're not looking
I pray that I never stop finding beauty in this love
That every day we are willing to put in the work to make our days
successful
Our weeks into months
Months into years
And one day we wake up old and grey
I want a forever love
I know I'm foolish for being such a hopeless romantic
But with you
Nothing ever really seems hopeless

There Are No Words I Can Write That Are More Beautiful Than This Moment

Us,
Me, right here, staring you in the eyes and giving you my heart
While fully acknowledging you are the very reason it beats
And I am okay with that
Today,
I vow to be honest with my emotions,
Even when they scare me
To let you love me,
Even the ugly parts
I vow,
To love you
Even on days I'm struggling to love myself
To always be fully here
In every moment I spend with you

You Are the Realest Depiction of God

I have ever seen
I say my prayers while you're asleep
And make sure to always kiss you before I leave your presence
Because you are my angel
And if ten years from now
I wake up with a broken heart
You are worth every piece of it
And I won't try and put it back together
Because you, you're it for me
If there is an after you
Call me stupid, but I never want to love again

You Are the Calm to My Storm

The eye holding me still when I'm spinning out of control
You are the twinkle in my smile
The stutter when I get excited
I am still wondering how something so powerful
can be so unassuming
How can u love me like you do?

To Say That I Love Him

Is to say that his happiness is my ultimate goal
That while I hope he receives that with me
I am content merely knowing he is happy
To say that I love him
Is to say that I am interested in seeing him become his best self
Is to say that I like the woman I am with him
To say that I love him
Is to take a risk
And trust that he is reward
That he is worth it all

Sometimes

I need you to grab me
To tell me that I'm good enough
That I didn't sell myself on a dream I don't deserve
Because I'm not sure what love is anymore
Because I'm not sure if it's fair to ask you to wait on me to be ready for
a commitment I already made
And it's not that I'm not sure about you
I'm just scared that I have been playing a role
Sold myself on practicality
Weighed the pros and cons of our love
Am I wrong for not wanting to settle?
For wanting a love that cannot be contained
That breaks glasses
And smears walls
That bursts

To Be Honest

I've never really worried that you're cheating
Call it arrogance
Naïveté
Or blind trust
But for some reason
I believe these vows meant something to you
That when you wrote them
You also burned them into the back of your brain
That when you placed the tattoo of my name right below your heart,
it was meant to be a reminder
That you could never stray too far without looking back
I'd be silly to say that your eyes will never wonder
Your thoughts meander to other women
But to be honest
When I come home at 1 am and you're still not here
I don't question your fidelity
I don't immediately jump to anger
But I wonder
Would you be this calm if I came home this late too
You see I'm the type of person that assumes that if you haven't called
or texted, it's because you're dead
And I know that sounds terrible
But I mean,
What else could be more important?
So now it's 2:42am
And I'm tired
But I can't sleep
'Cuz you're not here
I don't want to be that woman
That calls, that nags
Because you know how much faith I have in you
But it's irritating
And all I really want is some consideration
I'm tempted to get up
To go anywhere but here
Just so you can feel this

But that's not me
We both know that
But I wonder
How much pride do you give up for love?

"If there is any possible consolation in the tragedy of losing someone we love very much, it's the necessary hope that perhaps it was for the best."
– Paulo Coelho

It's Much Easier to Drown When No One Is Watching

To disappear when no one will notice
The very reason I fell in love with you is what makes this so hard
You have always seen me
Even when I did not want to be seen
I just feel like there are so many things I need to do
But I am stuck,
Underwhelming and unaccomplished
But you love me
You ride this wave, me
And I do not think that's fair
I have heard that the first year is the hardest
I pray it is not my fault

Sometimes I Get Overwhelmed

I kiss you and taste forever
Ironically, that taste lingers
I'm not sure if I like it or if I've just gotten used to it
You saw a lifetime from the moment you spotted me at the bar
Did my whispered hello warn you that I would always be shaky
ground?

I Keep Praying That You'll Love Me

Even when I'm not very lovable
I keep telling myself it doesn't matter
Because love can't save this
I keep biting back tears
After seeing things that remind me of the plans we'll probably never
fulfill
Do you remember when our love didn't hurt?
When sweet nothings were simply that,
Nothings
When they weren't spit out like consolation prizes
Used to fill the silence that keeps falling between us
Are you tired of the silence too?
Are you up right now?
Hurting
For what we've lost
For what's become so hard

I Have Since Been Wondering If You Felt It Too

The ground crumbing beneath us
Love is funny that way
You need it to build a relationship
But it can't sustain one

I Can Only Believe He Has Been Loved With Walls,

With conditions
So, he is not equipped with the tools to handle my demand for
unconditional

I Do Not Believe In Liars

Because I understand
Like flowers pressed into pages
That if you hold on to something long enough
Even you start to believe it's true
So, his truth
And the stories he tells me
Have become synonymous
He does not see what we've become
Sometimes
I want to meet him halfway
Apologize for things I may have made him do
Go back and stop myself from hurting him
But by this time,
The list is too long
He has learned to play the victim well
And I have grown sick of being the antagonist in his story

That Ring Getting Heavy

You used to be my fresh air, but now it seems like we're drowning
I'm good at being hurt
But better at being angry
I'm working on that
It's funny how quickly we fall
How soon the water rises
How we both swim to safety
But forget that we are each other's home
What does that mean?
If in crisis we still do not reach for each other?

I Wish I Could Change the Way Things Are Between Us

But I can't
I wish these tears didn't fall when we interact
But they do
I wish I could say things between us will change
But they won't
And the fact that this disease that is our relationship is terminal
Kills me
At first, I thought it was slowly
But the more we interact
The more pain I feel
The problem is you don't understand
You don't think it's real
And when you asked why I was crying
It hurt too much to say it was you
I realize there's no cure for this disease
Especially when both of us can't be pleased
And if we can't coexist together happy
Then I don't want to do it at all
I've learned the pain of climbing is nowhere near the pain of the fall

Yesterday I Felt Like Myself for the First Time in a While Now

Felt like I remembered where home was
Like I was yours
If only for a moment
I was happy
Felt like this ring that I have not worn in months deserved to be there
Like my finger was barren
Similar to my life without you
Yesterday we laughed and it felt genuine
I mentioned you without a lump in my throat
I felt like staying here
If only for a day

What's the Hardest Conversation to Have?

Telling your husband you're leaving him
Telling him that this world you've built together isn't good enough
Isn't what you envisioned
I once heard that divorce was like ripping your skin off
But it's more like
Relearning parts of yourself you told to be quiet
More like chasing every ounce of blood in your body and asking why
it still pumps for him
How do you mourn what died quicker than it began?
How do you not think yourself foolish?

The Short Answer

I loved myself too much to stay
I loved you too much to pretend
So I left

Today I Told a Stranger We Were Getting Divorced

I felt relieved after
Then slightly guilty
I have chosen not to think about what comes next
Or the moments I'll miss
The things we will no longer share
Instead I am focusing on myself
My power
My courage
In my ability to walk away from something
that no longer serves me

It Takes a Special Kind of Woman to Walk Away

To restart
To build herself from the ground up
Again
If we're being honest
I'm not her
And my heart keeps breaking, but I'm still hoping you'll catch the pieces
That after everything
You still think me yours
If we're being honest
I hate that about myself
Thought myself new age woman
Take no shit woman
Woman who loves herself enough that she does not need his too
But instead I am here
One foot in, one foot out
Halfway looking for what I know I have in you
But too stubborn to forgive
I wake up with regret
After a night spent pretending this doesn't hurt
That these men deserve me
That I even know what I deserve these days

I am Too Young

"To make something work"
To settle
Call me selfish
Call me quitter
Call it self-care

I'm Sitting in a 7/11 Parking Lot at 11pm

Texting a man that isn't you
Explaining to him that I can't give him something you already have
That I have nothing left to give to men
That I am tapped out
He wants exclusivity
Safety
To know that I won't leave
Or entertain other men
Ironic though
Because I guess you wanted the same thing
I have always been a hurricane
Beautiful from afar
But dangerous up close
I keep asking them to stay back
But they love the way the waves crash against the banks
Take solace in knowing that after destruction, the sun will still rise
They think I'm the sun
Completely unaware that I'm actually the storm

In a Perfect World

I could call you
And tell you I love you
And I'm sorry
For what, at this point, I don't even know
But it would erase all of this time
Of pain
Of misunderstandings
Because aren't you tired of hurting?
Of fighting?
Even if now the fights are silent?
Punches thrown like subtweets
And I only know because you haven't blocked me on Twitter yet
Or no need to call anymore
Ain't like you care anyway
If I was honest
I would tell you that I think you invited me into something you
weren't ready for
That I feel crazy for having standards so high
That I don't come around
Because hurt people hurt people
And I'd rather be by myself than continue hurting you
Ain't that love?

I Planned for Forever

I bet it's hard to believe that now
We had four kids
A destination wedding for our five-year anniversary
And happiness
Together
And nights like this are hard
When I can't sleep
And no one else feels worthy enough to talk to but you
But we don't talk anymore
And you wouldn't believe me if I said I missed you anyway

Reality Hurts Worse Than Paper Cuts

And today I realized I can only love you from afar
That I can no longer occupy the space I willingly chose to vacate
That divorce doesn't work that way
On the eve of receiving papers that will tell us who we are no longer
And you realizing your dreams may be a bit farther than you anticipated
I just want to love you
To hold you
To tell you that everything will be okay because I got you
Always have and always will
But you can't hear me over the sound of your breaking heart
Don't believe me while in the midst
And I guess I'm selfish for asking you to
But similar to the way my love didn't start when we said, "I do"
I don't think it will stop because I said, "I won't"

Cognitive Dissonance

Is it still called heartbreak if you're the one who broke it?
Do you still get to hold this pain?
If you're the one that walked away?
Will it mean I am a quitter?
That everyone was right?
Will it mean I am a terrible person?
I have never allowed myself to cry for this
For us
When you burn something to the ground
Are you allowed to mourn the ashes?
I am looking for exits again
Crafting my escape route
And I wonder
Do you find someone who makes you more of you?
Do you change for them?
Or do you simply quiet the voices in the back of your head
Is that what love is?

And Today, I am angry

Maybe it's because this man is not you
And no matter how hard I pretend, he doesn't make me feel like you
do either
Maybe it's because having two names is a bitch
And makes life really difficult
Maybe it's because I planned this life
And never once imagined it wouldn't turn out like I said it would
That my happily ever after wouldn't come true
Wouldn't be with you

To Admit That I Miss You

Is to say that I noticed your absence
Is to say that it is harder without you
Is to say that I need you
Is to say that I'm not sure you need me, too
After all
Here I am
Picking up the phone again
Calling you, first
Again
And this
This is a type of vulnerability I promised I wouldn't do anymore
Because I no longer want to compromise
And I don't want to know a love that hurts
Or continually asks me to swallow my pride
I can't keep choking for you

These Blank Pages Scare Me

Taunt me, waiting for words I am too scared to say
We have spent so much time salting this ocean between us
Fighting you is tiring
Pretending I don't miss you is worse
I am sorry
But I'm sure these apologies no longer hold weight

Do You Remember the Day We Said Forever?

Did you think it would come this fast?
Do you think my love fallacy?
Your time wasted
I don't know how to explain that I can no longer love you more than
myself
That you can give everything and still come up short
In these times
Words fail me
Emotions don't seem to move me like they should
Love doesn't seem to be enough
And I am scared that our memories will become invalid
That five years will be dwindled into the painful moments of goodbye
And I hope we're better than that

I'm Deleting Your Pictures Off Social Media Because That's What People Do In Breakups

And you've already blocked me from yours
So I guess I should follow suit
But an absence of pictures doesn't correlate to an absence in my heart
In my memories
And I'm scared that if I delete them all
I'll delete us
And maybe I already did when I left
But how do you erase something that you willingly allowed to be a part of your identity?
How do you start over without the person you wanted to end with?
How do you rebuild yourself?

I Spent a Couple Months Floating

Going from bed to bed searching for everything you promised me
And I'd leave unsatisfied
Because they weren't you
Didn't smell like you
Didn't feel like you
And some days
I fake it well
Laugh real loud
Smile real hard
But on days like this,
When 1000 people have told me happy birthday
I am simply waiting for you
I know I shouldn't feel this way because I walked away
But I left my heart with you

They Say You Think About Who You Love at 2am

And here I am thinking about you again
But I have never been confused of this fact
Never wanted my heart to know anyone but you
Yet you are no longer mine
Nor am I yours

I Wonder What You Say About Me When They Ask About Us

Do they..
Ask?
Or have you succeeded in completely erasing me,
Us
What we built
I know we ferociously tore it down
But even demolition sites still have traces of what was there
Will she see me in your eyes?
Will you hesitate to let her into a space I already
I mean,
Used to
Occupy
I tell people we are young
That I love you
That I wish you the best
I tell people that I miss you
But I think we are better apart
Right now
I tell them about the moment in five years when we bump into each
other at a coffee shop and we start over
About that love story
I tell them I'll never do matrimony again
.. Unless it's with you
I still tell them about you

"We gotta start teaching our daughters to be somebodies instead of somebody's."
– Kifah Shah

I Am Searching Myself

Trying to find the button
The reason I self-destruct every couple of years
Is it fair to ask you to keep rebuilding me?
Am I too proud to let you watch me crumble again?

Idolatry

I remember praying that I'd be a better partner to you before praying
I'd be a better person
I remember giving all I had to us
Before making sure I had anything to give
I am sorry
For making your words Psalm
And your kisses communion
I should have never deemed you perfection that way
And maybe I never said it aloud
Never asked you to be my deity
But I sang your praises often
Probably when you didn't deserve them
Kept resurrecting our love
As if it was bigger than us
Bigger than this world
I should have never loved you that way

I Was Someone's Daughter

Then someone's girlfriend
Followed by someone's wife
But never really remember being mine
Learning I was my own
Knowing myself without correlation

They Will Give You a Name

A label
Something to help them better understand such tragedy
Because you were supposed to fold
To break
To do anything but be standing here
So, they dismiss you with this name
Hand it to you
Seemingly like a consolation prize for besting a game you never asked
to participate in
You will hold this label
For some, it will be heavy
For others, it will feel like a badge of honor
Evidence that you didn't just make it all up
Proof that someone sees them
That someone believes them
But never forget you were something before this
That they don't get to name you
That you will be something after this
That this
Isn't the climax of your story
Not even the best chapter
It is your choice whether you hold on to this name
But living isn't the same as surviving
Living is so much more
You deserve that much

I See You

Trying your hardest to give what you don't have
Folding yourself over and over again to make room for him
To swallow him whole
Because maybe, just maybe
You'll be full that way
This yearning inside you will stop
If you complete each other
But how can you teach someone to love the parts of you, you have not
met yet
The parts of you, you refuse to acknowledge
And everything in between

Don't Ever Let Someone Tell You How You Should Be Loved

Or what you deserve
Or what you are worth
These things are yours and yours only
Some days you may aim too high
Some days you may aim too low
But these things are for you
Only you can decide
And you have every right to

I Am Still Learning to Love Myself Even When You Don't

That self-love cannot afford to be situational
I am still falling in love with me
Realizing every day may not be a happy one
And perfection is fool's gold
But every day is worth living
Every flaw of mine, still worth loving

I Hope You Know Their Inability to Love You Properly Does Not Mean You Are Unlovable

That sometimes people can only give what they have
What they know
And that may not be enough
Do not accept less than what you need
It is okay to walk away from things that do not serve you
Nor meet your standards
Keep your standards high
Protect your heart

Somedays

I am more Titanic than Coast Guard
Trying my hardest to survive
While telling everyone it will be ok

The Moment You Realize You Are Divorced

It will hit you
Kind of like a ton of bricks
That you are alone now
You will still be content with this decision because you have learned
that company for the sake of company does not equal companionship
That love is not magical
And it won't heal the wounds you've been inflicting upon yourself
Only you can fix that
And if success happens when no one's around to see it
It still exists

I Am Learning That Forgiving Myself Is the Hardest

Because isn't that what we're all afraid of,
Being responsible for our own demise?
Of crumbling in the face of adversity?
Of being said adversity?
Of being both hero and villain?

On Days When I See Nothing Staring Back At Me

I remind myself that bruised knuckles won't fix bruised hearts
That it's okay to be angry
But better to be honest
I come from people who trip on the word love
Mouths filled with shattered glass
Remnants of their broken hearts
And I vow to be better

I Have an Uncanny Ability of Standing

Even when life is trying its damnedest to knock me down
Of smiling
When all I truly want to do is break
Hide
From everything
But the thing about life is
It keeps going
Even on days you wish it wouldn't
On days when the clouds feel so low you're sure the darkness will
swallow you whole
But the sun will rise
Another day will come
And you will be there.
Still.

You Won't Realize How Far You've Come

Until one day
The pain won't be there anymore
It will be foreign
No longer comforting
It will be replaced with a smile
Or something more genuine
You won't know whether to label this feeling happiness
Because that is something that has always been fleeting for you
And you won't want to let this feeling go so easily
You will learn to be okay with being more firework than atom bomb
More bark than bite
This softness suits you
The weight of that armor was never yours to carry
You should have never had to protect yourself that way
Learning what love truly feels like will be a difficult process
It will mean unlearning the abuse that has tricked you for years
Unburying your heart
And trusting
This has never come easy for you
But I promise you are up for the challenge

At Some Point,

I became everything to everyone
And I forgot what it was like to just live
Forgot the necessity of honesty in authenticity
The beauty of reality
Because you can't save anyone
When you're drowning right next to them
And it's okay to acknowledge that this life vest is for you,
Today.

Honey,

You can choose your relationships
Choose who you let enter
Choose how you let people treat you
These lines no longer need to be fluid
You are still learning
You have only ever known a love that hurts
Love that stains
But is it always a good thing when love moves you to tears?
Are you afraid of change or afraid to lose him?
You've come so far
But you can't stop maturing
Choose to live in a world not motivated by anger
Or fear
Carve out your life
The way you want it to be
As naïve, utopic as that may be
TRY
Never stop trying
You're going to change the world
You just can't be afraid to

Here's to You

I don't think it's fair that you have to be alone or feel alone
Especially during the holidays
But I can't be there anymore
For my own sake
We have to learn what separate looks like
What separate feels like
All I know is that it still saddens me that things are the way they are
I haven't yet grown numb despite how hard I try to appear as such
I hope you're having a nice holiday
That you feel blessed
That you feel loved
If by no one else
Yourself
Know that even though we are not able to be together
My spirit is with you
Hoping
Praying
That you figure it out
That you heal from this
Here's to another year to get it right
Here's to acceptance
Here's to positivity
Here's to self love
Here's to you, one day.

Making Poets Immortal

www.310brownstreet.com

Made in USA - Kendallville, IN
24016_9780998427096
09.30.2022 1320